This library edition published in 2015 by Walter Foster Publishing,
a division of Quarto Publishing Group USA Inc.
3 Wrigley, Suite A
Irvine, CA 92618

Distributed in the United States and Canada by
Lerner Publisher Services
241 First Avenue North
Minneapolis, MN 55401 U.S.A.
www.lernerbooks.com

First Library Edition

Library of Congress Cataloging-in-Publication Data

Stacey, Nolon.
  Dogs & cats. -- First Library Edition.
     pages cm
  ISBN 978-1-939581-40-2
  1. Dogs in art. 2. Cats in art. 3. Drawing--Technique. I. Title. II. Title: Dogs and cats.
  NC783.8.D64S7278 2015
  743.6'97--dc23

                                                                    2013046831

012015
18582

9 8 7 6 5 4 3 2 1

Dogs & Cats

Whether you prefer the company of dogs, cats, or both, this essential drawing book will teach you how to create faithful depictions of all your furry friends. Inside, gifted artist Nolon Stacey provides fundamental techniques and complete instructions for drawing several different breeds of cats, kittens, dogs, and puppies. He also demonstrates how to portray specific canine and feline features—such as perky ears, wayward whiskers, and playful paws. Readers also will learn how to achieve accurate proportions and capture the priceless expressions that make dogs and cats so utterly irresistible! Packed with helpful tips and extraordinarily realistic drawings, this book is a "must-have" for every pet-loving artist.

CONTENTS

Walter Foster

TOOLS AND MATERIALS

The pencil is the most basic of all art media; you can get started with only a pencil and a piece of paper. I will recommend a few additional tools that I like to use, but over time every artist discovers the set of tools that works best for him or her. Experimentation is the key!

PENCILS

Artist's pencils are graded on a scale from soft (labeled "B" for "black") to medium (labeled "F" for "fine") to hard (labeled "H"). Softer leads create darker tones that are great for shading and blending; they also are much easier to manipulate with an eraser. Hard leads can produce light, fine lines, but avoid applying too much pressure as you stroke, as they easily can scar the paper's surface. There are 20 different grades of pencils, ranging from 9H to 9B. I don't believe it's necessary to buy all 20 grades; five or six spanning the range will suffice. I generally keep the following pencils on hand: 5B, 2B, HB, 2H, and 5H. As you purchase your set, just remember that the higher the number, the more exaggerated the quality (e.g., 9B is the softest available).

The most common pencil is the HB, which corresponds to the #2 pencil used in offices and schools. However, if I had to choose a single pencil to work with, I would opt for the 2B; this grade allows you to produce both very light tones and textures as well as near-black values, depending on the amount of pressure you apply.

In addition to grades of leads, there are many different types of pencils available. The most popular is the wooden pencil, which comprises a lead encased in a wooden sheath. The user can sharpen the pencil to a fine point for delicate lines or dull the point for broad lines or shading. I prefer a mechanical pencil (sometimes called a "clutch pencil"), which never needs sharpening. In contrast to wooden pencils, mechanical pencils do not change in weight or length, so you never need to adjust your feel for it. I use two types of mechanical pencils: one that holds a thin .2mm lead for a very fine point, and one that holds fatter .7mm lead for thick lines and fuller shading.

Types of Pencils You'll find that the material, shape, length, and weight of the barrel all affect your grip of the pencil. Test each type to see which feels most natural to you.

ERASERS

Erasers are invaluable art tools; in addition to removing mistakes, they can be used as drawing tools. There is a variety of eraser types available, and each has its own advantages. For example, you can create a highlight in hair by using the sharp edge of a hard vinyl eraser to lift out graphite. A pen eraser is similar to a large mechanical pencil but has an eraser core; to create a fine point for intricate erasing, simply use a conventional pencil sharpener. A kneaded eraser can be shaped into a fine point for detailed erasing, or flattened to gently lighten an area of graphite. My preferred eraser, tack adhesive, is a reusable putty that is moldable like the kneaded eraser but more effective at lifting graphite. You may also find an electric eraser handy for removing graphite quickly and easily.

PAPER

There are three main surfaces you can use for drawing: cold-pressed paper, which has *tooth* or a slightly raised texture; hot-pressed paper, which has a very smooth surface; and Bristol board (my preference), which is a fine-quality, heavyweight, smooth surface. The smoother the surface, the better suited for detail, as the tooth of rougher surfaces catches the graphite and makes it difficult to create smooth lines. Whatever type of surface you choose, use only archival, acid-free material that won't yellow or discolor over time.

BLENDING TOOLS

Use blending tools to smudge graphite, eliminate visible pencil strokes, merge dark tones into light, or smooth out textures. My favorite blending tools are tissues, paper towels, tortillons, and blending stumps. *Tortillons* and blending stumps are tightly wound sticks of paper. A tortillon is sharpened like a pencil at one end, whereas a blending stump is sharpened at both ends and is more tightly wound, producing a slightly different texture when rubbed on graphite. Chamois cloth also works well for achieving smooth blends. You should never blend with your finger; the skin leaves oils on the drawing paper, which can damage the surface or cause your shading to have an irregular tone.

ADDITIONAL TOOLS

There are a few more items you'll want to gather before you draw. I often keep a soft brush on hand for sweeping away bits of eraser or graphite from the paper, eliminating the temptation to use my hand. Contrary to what I was taught in art class, I use a ruler or straightedge when I need a perfectly straight line. Sometimes I even use a circle template for drawing pupils and irises when the subject is looking straight at the viewer. For indenting (a technique shown on page 6), I keep a knitting needle or empty mechanical pencil nearby. I also find a drawing compass useful for measuring and transferring proportions from a reference to my drawing. Another valuable tool for transferring an image to my drawing paper is transfer paper—thin sheets of paper that are coated on one side with an even application of graphite. Some artists like to keep a pencil sharpener on hand, but as I use mechanical pencils, this is unnecessary. I do keep a small piece of fine sandpaper nearby to resharpen tortillons or to blunt the end of a pencil, though. To shield areas of my paper from graphite or to anchor my drawing in place, I use artist's tape, which doesn't disturb the paper's surface. I also use a computer to display my reference photo.

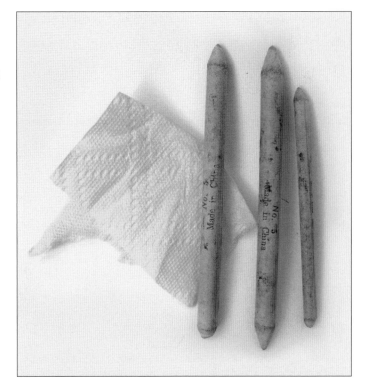

Choosing Tools Paper towels work well for large areas, but the range of blending stump and tortillon sizes allows you to work in large or small areas.

SETTING UP YOUR DRAWING SPACE

You don't need a studio—or even a drawing board—to start drawing. It is important, however, that you have a comfortable and well-lit space, preferably with natural light. Before I begin drawing, I lay out my work area, placing my artwork directly in front of me, my pencils to the right of the drawing (I am right-handed), and my remaining tools above the paper. Many artists prefer an easel, but I find that a flat surface provides better stability for my arm. When working from a photo, I often scan it and work while referencing the computer monitor, placing the computer directly in front of me, with my drawing paper on the table between the computer and me. This protects the photo from my graphite-covered fingers, and I can zoom in on areas of the reference.

Creating a Studio A studio can be located anywhere—from your home office to your kitchen table—but a north-facing room provides the best source of natural lighting.

DRAWING AND SHADING

Before you begin the projects in this book, it's important to understand the very basics of pencil drawing—from handling the pencil to blending and manipulating the graphite. These next pages feature a number of standard techniques that every pencil artist should be familiar with.

HOLDING THE PENCIL

I use two basic hand positions when drawing: the underhand position and the handwriting position. For the *underhand* position, I hold my palm almost parallel to the drawing surface with the pencil running under and across my palm. This places the lead at an effective angle to the paper for sketching, shading, and executing broad, sweeping strokes. For the *handwriting* position, I hold the pencil in the same way that I do for writing. I have the most control over the pencil in this position, and I can use the point for detailed and intricate work.

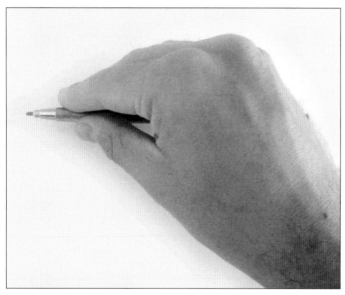

Underhand Position This is a useful position for sketching sweeping movements, such as those used for long hair.

Handwriting Position This position affords plenty of control for drawing fine details, such as facial features.

BLENDING

Blending can be used to create many textures, but it's particularly useful when you want smooth tones or subtle pencil strokes. Experiment with various techniques, and learn to choose your tools based on comfort and the size of the blending area.

Using a Tissue For an overall smooth effect, gently rub over an entire area with tissue.

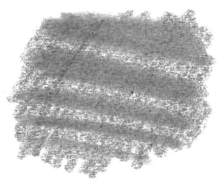

Using a Tortillon Tortillons can create lines over a large area, as shown, or smooth out tight areas.

GRADATING

You can create a shaded gradation (from light to dark or dark to light) by switching to a harder or softer pencil, respectively, or by gradually changing the pressure applied on the pencil. The harder you press, the darker the stroke will be. By creating scales like those shown below, you can see the range of *values* (the relative lightness or darkness of black) that various pressure amounts and pencil grades produce.

Value Scale: Changing Pencils This gradation of value begins with a 5B pencil, merges into a 5H, and finally ends with the white of the paper.

Value Scale: Smoothing the Tones For a seamless gradation, blend the tones with a tissue

BUILDING FORM

When drawing a dog or any other subject, two main elements create the form: shading and texture. The values used to shade an object describe its lightness or darkness relative to the light source; the variation in these values transform a flat image into artwork that appears three-dimensional. Texture also produces the illusion of form: Simply vary the value and density of your lines to render the texture, depending on the direction and strength of the light source—always keeping the lines nearest to the light source lightest and thinnest, and darkening and thickening them as they curve into shadowed areas.

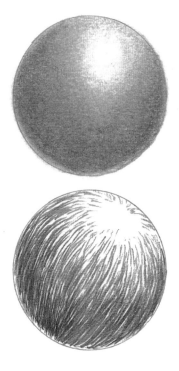

Creating Form with Shading By using darker values as you move away from the light source, you can give a sphere the appearance of form and depth. On the bottom sphere, the lines follow the contour of the curve; the darker and denser texture in the shadow areas communicate its form.

NEGATIVE DRAWING

Negative drawing means defining an object by filling in the area around it rather than the object itself. This method is particularly useful when the object in the foreground is lighter in tone than the background. Negative drawing is extremely helpful when drawing hair. You easily can draw dark hair using lines, but how do you draw light hair? You draw the negative shadows between the hairs.

Using Negative Drawing for Hair Once the negative space is shaded, you can add texture and tone to individual hairs to give them more realism and depth.

DRAWING WITH ERASERS

Erasers can produce a number of exciting effects when used with graphite. To create sharp highlights, use the edge of a hard vinyl eraser. To create a defined edge, simply shade roughly up to the edge of an object, and then run a hard eraser along the edge to eliminate any pencil strokes that run beyond it. You also can use an eraser to lighten objects, suggesting distance. First draw both near and far objects with exactly the same values; then form tack adhesive into a ball and roll it over the far objects until you achieve the desired contrast.

Drawing Lines with an Eraser Quickly stroking the edge of a hard eraser across graphite results in a clear line that can be used to suggest highlights.

Creating a Crisp Edge One long swipe of the edge of a hard eraser will define the edge of a shaded area, as seen on the right side of this example.

Drawing Hair To create this hair texture, apply a solid layer of shading. Then use the tip of an eraser to pull out short lines in the direction of hair growth.

FOCUSING ON FEATURES

Before creating a full canine portrait, it's a good idea to get to know the general shapes that make up each feature. As you practice rendering the features of a variety of dogs, notice the subtle changes in shape, value, and proportion that distinguish each breed.

EYES

The eyes are possibly the most important feature when it comes to capturing the personality and character of an animal. Below I provide a three-quarter view (turned slightly away from center).

Step 1 Using an HB pencil, begin by outlining the main areas of the eye—the pupil, the iris, the eyelids, and the highlight. Also sketch the hair around the eyes. Almost all dog breeds have a very dark area of bare skin surrounding the eyeball, so shade this area with solid tone.

Step 2 Next, using a 2B pencil, block in the darkest values of the eye, including the pupil (avoiding the highlight) and the area surrounding the eyeball. As you shade, leave small highlights in the corners of the eye to convey the impression of a moist, glistening surface.

Step 3 Begin creating the pattern of the iris using an HB pencil, drawing lines that radiate outward from the pupil toward the outer edge of the iris. Also use the HB pencil to add more hair around the eye, following the direction of growth.

Step 4 Finish the eye with an H pencil, adding more tone to the iris and then lifting out some graphite to indicate reflected light. Also soften the highlight with a tortillon. Then continue developing the hair, stroking over the top of the lid and over the outer corner.

EARS

Ears vary greatly in the canine world—they can be long or short, dropped or upright, and long haired or short haired. Here I provide an example of the upright ear of a German Shepherd Dog.

Step 1 The German Shepherd Dog has relatively large ears—especially given that they stand upright. In this example, we're viewing the dog's left ear straight on, so the shape is triangular. Begin by sketching the ear shape with an HB pencil, outlining the folds and mapping out some of the darker tones.

Step 2 Using a 2B pencil, begin adding hair to the ear, starting with the darkest hair around the base and along the uppermost edge. Let the hair dictate the form of the ear from now on, using very little shading. The hair grows upward and outward across the ear, with a hairless area along the inside flap of the ear.

Step 3 Go over the dark hairs with an HB pencil; this fills in the gaps with a slightly different tone, providing depth and thickness to the hair. Fill in most of the remaining gaps with strokes of a 2B pencil, applying very little pressure for the lighter areas. Finish by lightly shading the hairless area using a 2H pencil.

NOSES

There is a tremendous variation in size, shape, and even color of noses from one breed to the next. Below I'll draw a front view of the nose. Be sure to observe your subject from a variety of angles to truly understand the shape of its features.

Step 1 Begin by using an HB pencil to sketch the shape of the nose, including the nostrils. Be sure to study your subject and draw the shape you really see—not the shape you expect it to be. Then add rough guidelines to show where the main areas of light and shadow will be.

Step 2 Next add tone with a 2B pencil, using tiny circular strokes to emulate the unique texture of a dog's nose. Darken the nostrils and the vertical crease through the middle of the nose. Then begin shading the rest with lighter layers of circles. Leave the highlight areas free of graphite.

Step 3 Go over the entire nose with small circles to soften the texture slightly, but keeping the bumpy effect. Leave the top of the nose and the area under the nostril light to suggest the reflected light. To create the appearance of a wet nose, avoid blending the darks into the lights, instead allowing harsh separations.

Step 4 To connect the nose to the rest of the dog's face, begin adding the surrounding hair. As with the eyes, the hair grows away from the nose, with the darkest areas directly under and above the nose. The hair just below the nose is generally coarse, so keep these lines dark and short.

WHISKERS

There are a number of ways to suggest whiskers on your dogs—but keep in mind that many whiskers are light in color and often appear nearly translucent, so two of the three methods below and at right involve *not* drawing them.

Erasing Method For thicker whiskers, remove the graphite with the point of an eraser. This method is best suited for large or close-up drawings.

Indenting Method For light whiskers against dark hair, use a blunt tool to indent the whiskers; then shade over them. Continue the whiskers into lighter sections using a sharp HB pencil.

Negative Drawing Method To create thin or thick whiskers without disturbing the paper's surface, outline the parallel shapes of each whisker. Avoid stroking over them when adding hair.

RENDERING HAIR

The basic categories of dog hair are long and curly, long and straight, short and curly, and short and straight. Roughness or smoothness of the hair also affects its appearance. There are many variations within each basic type of hair, but you should be able to adapt one of the techniques demonstrated in this section to draw any dog hair you wish. For the longer hair types, I'll show both a detailed method with definite areas of shadow and highlight and a quicker, sketchier method created simply with lines.

LONG, CURLY HAIR

DETAIL METHOD

Step 1 Long, curly hair tends to flow in waves. Begin drawing wavy lines using an HB pencil, roughly following a consistent pattern of curvature while ensuring that the pattern isn't too rigid and exact. Be sure to overlap some hairs for realism.

Step 2 Darken the areas in between the main clumps of hair using a soft pencil. Then suggest the strands within the clumps of hair nearest the viewer, using long strokes to communicate the length. Leave some areas nearly free of graphite to bring them forward visually.

SKETCH METHOD

Step 1 To draw the same hair with a freer, looser style, don't worry about positioning the hairs or other details; just sketch long, wavy lines, again following a general S-shaped pattern.

Step 2 Now rough in texture using lines. Rather than creating definite areas of highlights and shadows, simply place the lines closer together in shadowed areas and farther apart in lighter areas. When drawing any type of hair, always stroke in the direction of growth.

LONG, STRAIGHT HAIR

DETAIL METHOD

Step 1 Long, straight hair doesn't necessarily lay in perfectly parallel lines. In fact, the longer the hair, the more haphazard it's likely to be. With this in mind, draw long sections of hair, stroking in different directions and overlapping strokes.

Step 2 Carefully shade the dark areas among the hairs, and apply long, light strokes on top of the sections of hair. Then use tack adhesive to lift out some individual hairs, giving depth to the coat.

SKETCH METHOD

Step 1 Draw light, rough lines to provide guidelines for the sections of hair. Then use long, wispy strokes to gradually build up the strands along the guidelines. Place lines closer together for dark areas and farther apart for light areas.

Step 2 As with the detailed method, add highlights and depth by lifting out additional hairs using tack adhesive formed to a point.

SHORT HAIR

Short, Straight Hair From a Dalmatian to a Doberman Pinscher, many breeds have coats with short, straight hair. This is the simplest type of hair to draw, as it generally is made up of only short lines. For a detailed rendering, draw many straight lines, all running in the same direction (in this example, on a diagonal). To give the impression of individual short hairs, draw pairs of lines, tapering the ends together to form a point for each hair. Keep your strokes quite free; try not to think about each hair, but let your hand randomly draw the lines.

Short, Curly Hair A few breeds, such as Poodles and Bichon Frises, have coats with short, soft, tight curls. A good way to draw this type of hair is to fill the area with even shading using an HB pencil, then blend with a tissue. For the highlights, use an eraser to lift out graphite using a random, circular motion. In this view, the light is coming from above, so the shadows are on the underside of each highlighted curl.

OTHER TYPES OF HAIR

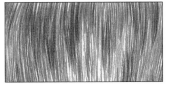 

Smooth Hair To draw the smooth, silky hair of a Yorkshire Terrier or Afghan Hound, you must make your strokes more uniform. Unlike the long hair of a Golden Retriever, the shiny hair of a Afghan Hound lays very straight. Draw long, sweeping, parallel lines, leaving lighter areas for highlights. As with any type of hair, avoid drawing the lines too uniformly in direction or value, which produces an unnatural look.

Fluffy Hair A puppy's hair is generally fluffier than a mature dog's hair. I've found that the same method I use for short, curly hair works well for puppies, although it will not work for every breed. Another approach is to create rough rows of hair that give the impression of hair fluffing outward, as shown above. Draw lines close together, following rows across the paper, and make some strokes longer than others to break up any distracting patterns.

CATS IN A BAG

Step One With so much of the cats' bodies obscured by the bag, this is a relatively simple drawing. I don't have to worry much about the accuracy of their bodies, so I create the outline freehand. I begin by drawing the bag, and then I place the facial features and indicate the main areas of fur. I include plenty of detail in the outline, which saves me from having to assess the placement of elements as I progress. I even indicate the serrated edge of the bag.

Step Two I indent the cat's whiskers before shading to preserve the white of the paper. Then I begin picking out all the black areas of the drawing, blocking them in with a 2B pencil. This involves some negative drawing, which simply means that I shade around the clumps of hair. The fact that I sketched these hairs as part of the line drawing makes this process much simpler.

Step Three I now block in the main shading of the bag using a blunt HB pencil. As I apply tone to the bag, I leave the outer edge white to help create the illusion of contrast between the cats and the bag. To model the folds and crinkles on the bag, I lift out the raised areas with an eraser and darken areas of shadow across the surface. I also add a cast shadow under the bag using the HB pencil.

Step Four Now I address the hair on the cat at left. Beginning with the markings on the forehead, I use 2B and HB pencils to create the darker and lighter hairs, respectively. Stroking in the direction of hair growth, I move upward in the middle of the head and curv outward as I move toward the sides. Using fairly random lines, I flick some hairs off cours for realism. As I get closer to the bag where the hair is in shadow, I am conscious to darke my strokes. Using this same shading method, I move across the rest of the cat's face and down onto its paws. I've already negatively drawn the darks around the paws, so I simply block in this lower area using an HB pencil. I then go over it again with a 2B pencil to add texture and create clumps of hair. I also block in the iris using an HB pencil.

Step Five I finish the first cat by using an H pencil to draw fairly light lines within the fur, adding texture to the white area of the face. I also darken the area where the top lip overlaps the bottom, and I apply small circles over the nose for texture. I apply more pressure to the pencil at the sides of the nose and toward the bottom to create form. I also add the dark whisker markings on the cheeks.

Step Six I use the exact same process to shade the next cat. I want the cat at right to be slightly lighter than the cat at left, so I leave more white paper showing through my pencil lines as I progress. I constantly turn to my reference image so I can accurately re-create the markings in my drawing, changing from the HB to the 2B pencil for the darker markings.

▶ **Step Seven** I use *block shading* (applying an even layer of graphite over an area) on the bottom half of the second cat using an HB pencil and begin to create gaps between clumps of hair using a 2B pencil. These are lines that I apply fairly randomly to change the direction of hair growth. Finally, I stroke over these clumps of hair using a sharp eraser to lighten them slightly. I also define the hairs of the cat's chin using the same eraser. To complete the drawing, I use an electric eraser to further define some of the whiskers.

BULLDOG

▶ **Step One** I sketch the outline of the head using an HB pencil, placing it slightly to the right and above the middle of my drawing area. I add the arch indicating the muzzle, the shape of the jowls, and the eyes, adjusting until I achieve accurate proportions. Very little of the body is showing, so it is quite simple to sketch the shoulders, front paws, and what little of the rear body is visible. I now refine this sketch so I have definite areas to begin shading, delineating them with strokes that follow the direction of hair growth.

Step Two I lighten my initial sketch with a putty eraser (also called "adhesive putty") and then use a 2B pencil to block in the darkest areas, which include the eyes, nostrils, and slightly open mouth. Then I apply a layer of HB graphite to each eye, lightening the tone as I move toward the bottom edges to give them a spherical look. I leave the highlight free of tone. I finish by darkening the skin around the eyes and then complete the right eye in the same manner. I also create texture on the nose by drawing random cracks over a layer of tone using a 2B pencil. Notice how the cracks in the middle of the nose all point away from the nostrils and middle crease, giving the illusion of curvature in this area.

Step Three Now I move on to the hair. Bulldogs have a fairly short, coarse coat, so I will be using short pencil strokes throughout the body. I begin with the darkest areas of the head, which are the skin folds and shadows within the ears. Using a 2B pencil, I apply short strokes in the direction of growth. The hair always grows away from the eyes in a slight spiral shape, moving up over the head and out toward the ears, and also down the side of the muzzle and out toward the side of the face. Remembering this pattern makes the early stages easier. These short lines not only provide me with the darkest areas, but they also create smaller, more manageable areas on the face that I can address one at a time.

Step Four Switching to an HB pencil, I use the same short strokes to add the hair spiraling away from the eye. I intentionally leave areas of paper showing through my lines, which I then go over with a 2H pencil to create the lightest hairs. I continue this process over the rest of the head. The darker 2B lines that I applied earlier are now showing through the lighter HB lines, giving the impression of folds and ridges of fur. For the white patch on the forehead, I merely stroke a few short lines with an H pencil to indicate light hair.

Step Five The muzzle is slightly trickier—this area features very short white hairs and black skin beneath. I create this look using very short pencil strokes, leaving white between the hairs. The area directly below the nose and the lower lip is almost free of hair, so I indent a few stray hairs and then shade it using a 2B pencil. Then I apply a few stroke of HB for more white hair on the muzzle and along the tops of the ears.

▶ Step Six I finish the ears with a layer of HB. The inside of the ear has ridges but no hair. I apply more pressure to either side of the ridges and then add a highlight to the top of the ridge using a putty eraser. Now I'm ready to work on the body. The darkest area is the shadowed underside, so I apply block shading here first, avoiding the white of the chest. I work exactly the same way as I did on the face, applying the darker lines first to produce the folds of fur and progressing to lighter lines. It is very important that you study your reference image to follow the direction of hair growth.

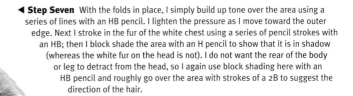

◀ Step Seven With the folds in place, I simply build up tone over the area using a series of lines with an HB pencil. I lighten the pressure as I move toward the outer edge. Next I stroke in the fur of the white chest using a series of pencil strokes with an HB; then I block shade the area with an H pencil to show that it is in shadow (whereas the white fur on the head is not). I do not want the rear of the body or leg to detract from the head, so I again use block shading here with an HB pencil and roughly go over the area with strokes of a 2B to suggest the direction of the hair.

▶ Step Eight All that remains now are the paws, which I want to be detailed like the head (as they are in the foreground). I shade the nails, first applying a dark edge to each using a 2B pencil. Then I add a thick line using a blunt HB pencil along the dark edge, leaving the rest white to indicate reflected light. I shade the undersides of the pads using an HB pencil; then I apply the graphite using very small circles to imply a rough texture. Next I begin building up the layers of fur on the paws with a 2B pencil, applying the lines closer together in the shadows, such as between the digits. Finishing the paws is as simple as applying a single layer of HB pencil over the entire area to indicate the value of the brown hair. Finally, I ground the dog with a subtle shadow. I apply a little graphite with a 2B pencil under the body and each of the paws, and then I blend with a tortillon.

Dachshunds

Step One When drawing two similar dogs, like these two Dachshunds, it is important to identify and translate the differences between them. You don't want to end up with a drawing of two dogs that look identical. With this in mind, I work on both dogs simultaneously. I begin by marking out the general shape of the dogs using circles to represent the bodies and heads. Then I add rough shapes for the muzzles, ears, and legs. I want the two dogs to be looking at the same thing, but again I don't want them to look like the same image duplicated, so I slightly lower the muzzle of the dog on the right. Different positioning of the ears also helps distinguish the two.

Step Two I now fine-tune my outline to provide a better idea of the dogs' structures. First I erase all the internal lines that aren't required, leaving just the outline of the dogs. Then I add the facial features and identify the main markings of the coats. I don't want any harsh lines that may show through later, so I use a putty eraser to lighten my line drawing until I can hardly see it. I then use it as my basis for creating a much more detailed line drawing. I mark out the main areas of hair using lines in the direction of growth. The chest is quite complex in terms of how the direction of hair growth changes, so I carefully refer to my photo reference for guidance.

Step Three Now I block in the darkest areas of the dogs using a 2B pencil. I begin with the blacks of the nostrils and the eyes, leaving the highlights free of tone. Then I section off the areas of dark hair by simply indicating the edges with strokes that follow the direction of hair growth. I then fill in these areas with a 2B pencil, still stroking in the direction of hair growth and tapering each stroke as it moves toward the edge of the section. In this stage, I ignore any areas that do not appear black.

Step Four Now I begin blocking in some of the larger areas of fur. I accomplish this in two stages (steps four and five). Using a 2B pencil, I apply fairly short and very dark lines over the tops of the heads, across the muzzles, and down the necks. I place the lines closer together in darker areas, such as the below the eyes, and farther apart in lighter areas, such as the tops of the heads. At this point, the white of the paper still shows between the lines, so it looks too harsh.

Step Five The second stage involves applying a fairly dark layer of graphite over the lines to soften the look of the coats. As this is black hair, I stick with the 2B pencil to achieve a dark layer, but I am careful not to apply too much pressure—I still want the lines from steps three and four to show through. As I apply these layers, I avoid the two "brown" spots on the sides of the faces and the lighter hair behind the eyes. Then I switch to an HB and apply a lighter layer of graphite over these areas.

Step Six I repeat this two-stage process of applying dark lines followed by a layer of shading across the necks and shoulders. Then I address the chests using a 2B pencil, applying sparse guidelines in the direction of hair growth. With this hair growing in all different directions, it would be very easy to end up with a section of hair that looks very unnatural, so it's important to roughly map out the flow of the hair. There are essentially three crowns on the chest from which the hairs spread: one in the middle of the chest and two above the legs. The hair spirals from these crowns up to the neck and down to the stomach.

Step Seven With these hair-growth guidelines in place, I am now confident that I can accurately add the dark lines of the chests. I do this using a 2B pencil and tapered strokes. The lines all originate from the crowns of the hair and blend into the existing strokes. You can see that this has provided the shape and structure of the chests—even without shading.

Step Eight The lower legs and paws are covered with brown hair—not black—so I layer these lighter areas with an HB pencil. I use the same pencil to apply strokes over the "brown" muzzles and jaw areas of the dogs. I start near the tops of the muzzles and lighten the pressure as I move down over the cheeks, as the light hits these areas more directly. I draw the dark whisker markings, darken the shadows between the lips, and add a crease where the skin stretches to the side just below the mouth. I add whiskers with long, curved strokes using an HB pencil. Finally, I use a 2B pencil to ground the two floating Dachshunds with simple cast shadows beneath them.

KITTENS

Step One Because my drawing will be relatively small (approximately 8 1/2 x 10 inches) and my reference is not a close-up photo of the kittens, I use a "sketch" method of drawing. I begin with a rough line drawing to ensure that I have my proportions correct, erasing and adjusting the lines as necessary. I include the general shape of the kittens, the features, the ears, and some rough guidelines for the main fur markings.

Step Two Once I have positioned the features accurately, I lighten my line drawing with a putty eraser to the point where I can barely see it. I use this as a guide for creating a much more detailed line drawing. (If I were to try to draw these two cats in detail without this initial guide, I would most likely lose touch of the proportions.) In this drawing, I detail the features, show the main markings on the coats, and indicate the direction of fur growth. This early sketch allows me to concentrate solely on tone and texture later.

Step Three With my final sketch in place, I indent the whiskers before adding any tone to the face. Then, to simplify the drawing at an early stage and visually break up the white paper, I begin shading by filling in the darkest areas of the kittens using a 2B pencil. After filling in the pupils and skin around the eyes, I quickly add the dark markings of the heads, the shadow between the kittens, and the areas of the body where the hair separates. To create these dark strands of hair, I loosely draw my lines using a back-and-forth motion. I ignore any hair that doesn't appear completely black in the reference.

Step Four Before continuing work on the fur, I address the features. I simply block in the eyes using a blunt HB pencil, avoiding the highlights; then I add radial lines around the pupils using a sharp HB pencil. I shade the nose using an H pencil and small circles. Now I return to the fur, starting with the cats' foreheads. I have already applied the darkest markings, so I simply go over the areas using an HB pencil, stroking in the direction of hair growth. I draw medium-length lines leading up the heads and out toward the ears. At this stage, I make sure to leave the white of the paper showing through between the lines.

Step Five I create the whisker markings using a 2B and then shade around them using an HB pencil to suggest the subtle parting of fur. Now I work fairly quickly and spontaneously on the fur. Using strokes in the direction of fur growth, I work across the areas under the heads using an HB pencil. As I work away from the heads, I lighten my strokes slightly. Switching to an H pencil, I layer lighter strokes into the cheek areas. I continue this process across the body of both kittens, working from dark to light. I apply more pressure and place my lines closer together as I move toward the outer edge of each kitten, flicking the pencil outward to create the fluffy edge of fur. I also very roughly add some texture to the legs and paws; I will refine this in the next step.

Step Six Now I use a tissue to lightly blend the fur of each cat. I avoid only the areas surrounding the eyes and nose, as I want these to remain pure white. This blending not only softens the slight harshness of my lines, but it also creates the midtone fur across each cat's entire body.

▶ **Step Seven** Now I use a sharply cut eraser to lift out some of the white fur that I lost by blending, focusing on the chests and the fronts of the legs. To add the white whiskers, I use the eraser as I would a pencil. Where the whiskers extend beyond the fur, I apply fine lines of an H pencil. Finally, I create a cast shadow using a blunt 2B and blending with a tissue.

15

CAT PORTRAIT

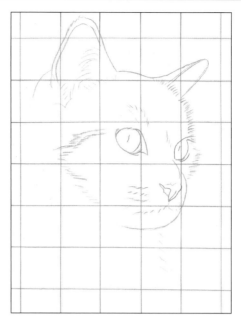

Step One I want this portrait to be very detailed and accurate, so I use the grid method to create my initial outline drawing. I begin by drawing a one-centimeter grid on a printout of my reference image (I don't want to damage the original photo).

Step Two Then I lightly draw a three-centimeter grid on my drawing paper using a 2B pencil (harder pencils can indent the paper and show through on the finished piece). This will enlarge the reference photo to three times the original size. Once I have my grid in place, I simply work through each square, transferring as much detail as I can from the reference to my paper.

Step Three Now I completely erase any traces of my grid and redraw any parts of my line drawing that have been erased in the process. Some people prefer to erase their grid as they progress, but I prefer to start with a line drawing that is as clean as possible. I do not want to be distracted by squares during the shading process.

Step Four As I often do, I begin by picking out the darkest areas (the nostrils and eyes) using a 2B. Notice that the pupils aren't the usual "cat" shape; because the cat's head is turned from the viewer, they appear almost as lines. To complete the iris, I use an HB pencil to fill in the eyeball with a midtone, leaving the highlights white. I then create radial lines emanating from the pupil. For the nose, I simply fill in the shape using an HB pencil, darkening slightly as I move toward the bottom.

Step Five With the eyes and nose complete, I look at the expanse of white paper in front of me and feel quite intimidated. To break up the drawing into more manageable sections, I create some solid breaks within the fur on the head, beginning with the dark "C" shape across the cheek. For this I use a 2B pencil, first pressing quite hard to create some very dark gaps in the hair and then lightening the pressure for slightly lighter fur. I also add shading above the cat's right eye, at the base of the ear, and at the back of the head. Switching to an HB pencil, I use short lines to add the fur under the eye and up to the "C."

Step Six I apply a layer of HB graphite over the cheek are to blend the strokes, softening the darks and eliminating the white of the paper showing through. I work my way down with the H pencil to indicate the line of the mouth, stroking in the direction of hair growth. I use a 2B pencil for the darker hairs of the mouth as well as the whisker markings. Then I layer short strokes of an HB pencil over the mouth. (I don't concern myself with whiskers yet—I wil erase them at the end.) Using my 2B pencil, I create tiny "V" shapes over the forehead; the white showing through gives the impression of tapering hairs.

Step Seven I finish the rest of the fur on the head using the same method as I used on the cheek. The hair is quite contrasting with lots of very dark areas mixed in with lighter hair. As I move toward the back of the head with the 2B pencil, I don't concern myself with detail. I want this area to appear out of focus, directing the viewer back to the face of the cat. Then I indent the long hairs in front of the insides of the ears; this will save me from having to draw around the hairs when I shade these areas.

Step Eight I fill in the inside of each ear using an HB pencil. The impressed hairs remain free of tone. Now I get the collar in place before moving on to the chest. Whenever a collar is present in a reference photo, I like to include it. I find that it adds interest and can personalize a drawing. I shade what little of the collar is showing using a 2B pencil, drawing up into the hair laying over it. I draw the dark shadows of the metal tag using a 2B pencil and shade the smooth, shiny surface with a 2H pencil, blending it with tissue. I simply write the cat's name, Mister, with a sharp H pencil, leaving white edges to give it an engraved appearance. Then, using the H pencil, I lay down a light shadow pattern on the white hair of the cat's chest.

◄ **Step Nine** I finish the rest of the chest in two stages. First I lay down the darker areas created by partings in the hair. Then I indent some stray hairs to save time and ensure that all the white won't become covered with graphite. I want the drawing to fade out toward the bottom, so I don't include much detail along the edges; I simply block shade with an H pencil. Finally, I block shade the entire chest using a blunt HB pencil, and I blend the graphite using tissue to fade out the tone along the bottom. To bring a little detail to the area, I use a sharp vinyl eraser to cut in some lighter hairs. To complete the drawing, I add whiskers using an electric eraser, curving each one out in a single stroke from the whisker markings on the cheek. For the whiskers at left, I use curving strokes and an H pencil.

SPRINGER SPANIEL PUPPY

▶ **Step One** I begin by transferring the basic outline of the pup using an HB pencil and transfer paper. I trace only the most basic outlines to ensure that the proportions are accurate and every feature is positioned as it is in the reference photo. Then I refine the outlines to suggest the pup's hair, erasing the transferred lines as necessary. Using short, tapering strokes, I indicate the direction of hair growth across the figure. I also refine the outlines of the eyes and nose.

▶ **Step Two** I use a 2B pencil to block in the pup's pupils, working around the highlight. I also add the thin lines of dark skin around the eyes. Then I use the same pencil to begin developing the darkest areas of hair around the eye socket, around the face, within the ears, and down the back, always stroking in the direction of hair growth. I vary the length of each stroke to keep the hair from looking too uniform, and I taper them to build the groundwork for seamless transitions between values.

▶ **Step Three** After I've addressed the darkest areas with tone, I increase the value by stroking over them with a 4B pencil. I pay close attention to the curving and swirling patterns within the hair. Returning to the 2B pencil, I stroke within the ears to define strands of hair, focusing on the shadows. The new strokes follow the direction of the previous strokes and blend easily to create the illusion of wavy hair. I also apply a layer of tone to the nose using light, circular strokes.

▶ **Step Four** Now I use an HB pencil to apply the lightest tones to the dog's ears. I stroke alongside the previous layers of graphite, creating a soft, silky look. I also develop the eyes and nose, adding midtones and pulling out highlights where needed. I use the 2B pencil to pull tone over the light areas of the body, connecting the sections of hair. I also begin developing the hair over the dog's face, scooping under and over the eyes to follow the direction of hair growth.

▶ **Step Five** Using a blunt but fine metal point, I impress lines for the pup's whiskers. As I develop the fur over the whiskers, the impressed areas stay free of graphite. I also build up tone over the Spaniel's back using a blunt 2B pencil.

▶ **Step Six** With an HB pencil, I indicate the hair on the pup's muzzle, keeping some areas white as I stroke. I follow my reference carefully so that I can re-create the pup's facial markings and produce an accurate likeness. Then I move on to the markings within the white areas of the pup's coat. I use a 2B pencil and merely suggest the direction of hair growth with minimal strokes, adding curves, sprouts, swirls, and spots according to the photo reference.

▶ **Step Seven** With an H pencil, I add fine strokes to develop the area of white hair. Then I use a tissue to gently rub over areas in shadow, focusing on the pup's underside. I also add a light layer of graphite to serve as a soft cast shadow under the pup, blending the strokes with a tissue.

Husky

Step One This Husky is in a striking stance, so I aim to capture its powerful look in my drawing. I decide to include a dark background so the light, fluffy coat of the Husky stands out on the paper. (Remember that lighter dogs run the risk of getting lost in the white of the paper.) I begin by sketching a rough outline of the Husky. I don't refine the sketch because I'll put in the background first—I can fine tune the outlines later. However, I make sure to position the features accurately. I also mark the folds of skin that help indicate the twist in the upper body.

Step Two I block in the background using a blunt 5B pencil, working around the shape of the dog. I apply more pressure as I move toward the bottom. I don't want a detailed background that will take away from the dog, so I keep it abstract. In my reference, the dog's upper body is darker than the lower body and legs; I counter this by using a background that gradates from dark moving up to light. To add interest, I use a putty eraser to stroke rough lines at the top of the drawing, giving the impression of a sky. I also add subtle shadows near the dog's legs. I use a pencil eraser to flick out around the edge of the dog, suggesting fluffy fur.

Step Three Now I start working on the dog. First I pick out the darkest areas and shade them with a sharp 2B pencil. These include the eyes and nose which, at this distance, don't require much detail. Then I move on to the dark fur of the head and back, simply using random, zigzagging lines. Returning to the head, I use a sharp 2B pencil and fairly short lines to develop the hair up and over the forehead and out toward the ears. The Husky has light areas around the eyes, so I leave these white for now.

Step Four I now switch to an HB pencil and go over the dark fur of the head with more short lines, following the same direction as used in step three. I then block shade over the areas of dark hair using a blunt 2H pencil to add tone and eliminate the white of the paper. This method of applying 2B, then HB, and finally 2H pencils gives the fur a sense of great depth. I repeat this technique over the back of the dog, applying my lines closer together where my guidelines indicate creases in the coat.

▶ **Step Five** Moving to the dog's back, I repeat my technique of adding HB and 2H lines over the 2B strokes. I extend the layer of 2H pencil down over the thigh, creating a lighter tone of fur. I also erase some lines of hair on the underside of the dog and where the stomach meets the hind leg. I block in the fur of the hind legs using an HB pencil, making sure that the tones differ from those of the surrounding background. I erase the back edge of each leg to suggest reflected light.

▶ **Step Six** I now focus on the front of the dog. The coat here is much lighter than across the body, so I use the same technique as in previous steps. However, instead of starting with the lines of a 2B pencil, I start with the lines of an H pencil. Then I move to the 2H and layer over the top with the blunt side of a 2H pencil. I leave the white of the paper showing though where the light is hitting the back of the legs and the dog's front right shoulder.

▶ **Step Seven** As I continue across the neck, I minimize detail in this area so the Husky's face stands out. I simply use an HB pencil and begin filling in the area with strokes in the direction of hair growth, applying the lines closer together to create creases in the coat. I switch to a 2B pencil for the neck area at left, where the coat is in shadow. My lines are slightly longer here, as the fur lengthens around the neck.

▶ **Step Eight** I now go over the neck with a blunt 2H pencil to blend the area, and then I pick out the highlights using a pencil eraser. The main highlights are just to the left of the muzzle, where clumps of fur are catching the light. I also blend along the left edge of the neck where it is almost completely in shadow. Then I use an HB pencil to shade the remaining parts of the face and ears. The shadows of the face include the inner corner of the eye, under the eye, along the base of the muzzle, and down the dog's cheek. I roughly shade these areas using very little detail. I then darken the back sides of the ears, which are also in shadow, using a 2B pencil. To finish, I erase the top of the muzzle to create more contrast within the face.

SILVER TABBY

Step One I begin by roughly sketching the general shape of the cat using an HB mechanical pencil. This cat's pose makes for quite a simple outline, as we have no legs to worry about—just the mound of the cat's back, the neck, and the head. I include the ears and features of the face to ensure that I have everything correctly positioned. I use the ears as a guide to align the eyes and line of the mouth.

Step Two When I am happy with the layout and proportions of my rough sketch, I can fine-tune the sketch. I erase my rough outline until I can barely see it, and I use it as a guide for building details, such as the features, outline, and fur markings. I prefer that my outlines follow the direction of hair growth so they won't show through in the final drawing.

Step Three I am now ready to begin shading the cat's fur. I approach this drawing a little differently than usual. As the cat's back is mostly black with patches of gray and lighter fly-away hairs, I first indent the fly-away hairs using an empty mechanical pencil so that they will remain white through my later shading. I then use a similar method of indenting with a hard pencil. Using a sharp 5H pencil, I draw all the light hairs of the cat's back that appear in the darkest areas. I apply quite a lot of pressure, which slightly indents the paper while creating the light line. This method allows me to simply shade over these areas; the indented lines and 5H lines will show through.

Step Four As you can see, I have shaded over all but the lightest areas of the back using strokes with a sharp 2B pencil. My earlier indenting has now resulted in the cat having three tones of hair: the black, the light 5H, and the indented hairs that are left as the white of the paper. I flick my pencil outwards at the end of every stroke so as to avoid any harsh edges to my shading. This will make blending the dark areas into the light areas much easier later.

Step Five I now switch to an HB pencil and fill in the remaining areas of the back. These areas are the lighter parts of the back so I keep my strokes quite far apart, allowing the white of the paper to show through in between. I vary the angle of my lines only slightly while following the direction of hair growth. This slight variation creates clumps of diverging and parting hair.

Step Six As the cat is black and silver, I want to soften the white of the paper that is still showing through by covering the entire area with a layer of H graphite. The only hairs that now appear white are the fly-away hairs that we indented at the start. Applying this layer at this stage, rather than earlier, also has the benefit of blending the graphite that is already there, softening some of the harsh lines.

Step Seven I continue up the neck to begin defining the area around the face. The hair of the neck is gray in color, so I use a blunt H pencil and block shade the left side of the neck. I leave a few white areas where the light is catching the fur. I switch back to the 2B pencil to darken the area that defines the cheek and use zigzag lines to create the appearance of fur.

Step Eight I use the same mix of H and 2B pencil strokes over the rest of the face, creating the markings with zigzagging strokes of a 2B and blocking in the lighter hair with a blunt H pencil. The insides of the cat's ears are slightly darker but have light hairs growing over them. I block shade this area using an HB pencil and then erase the lighter hairs with the sharp edge of an eraser. Then I define the mouth with a dark shadow, gradually lightening toward the bottom of the chin.

Step Nine I fill in the rest of the cat's face using an HB pencil and a series of short lines. I simply apply more pressure with the HB to create the darker areas and lighten my pressure for the light areas. Note how the hair grows out from the eyes toward the sides of the face and up toward the ears.

▶ **Step Ten** Now the only remaining areas are the eyes, nose, and whiskers. As always, I use a 2B pencil to block in the darkest areas—the nostrils, the pupils, and the skin surrounding the eyes. I leave a white highlight across each pupil to enhance the moist appearance of the eye. Then I block shade the eyes and nose with an H pencil, switching to an HB pencil to apply a series of lines radiating from the pupil. Now I darken the bottom, top, and central crease of the nose to suggest its form. Because the viewer sees the cat from behind, I feel that the cat is grounded well enough and doesn't need a cast shadow. Finally, I add the whiskers. Using a pencil eraser cut to a sharp edge, I erase the whiskers starting from the whisker markings and sweeping out and downward. I do this on both sides of the face, but I finish the whiskers on the cat's left side with an H pencil so they stand out against the white background.

DALMATIAN

▶ **Step One** I begin by sketching the general shape of the Dalmatian's head using an HB pencil. As this is a relatively simple head shot, I can sketch the outline without needing to block in shapes or use a grid. I make sure to capture the tilt of the head, which gives this dog great character. I ensure that the tops of the ears, eyes, and line of the mouth are all parallel and follow this tilt. I also roughly mark in some of the spots.

▶ **Step Two** Once I am happy with my outline, I begin blocking in the darkest areas using a 2B pencil. Although there are many black spots on this dog, I do not want to block in each black patch entirely, as areas of the coat still reflect light. In addition to the spots, I block in the pupil, the dark outline of the eyes, and the nostrils.

▶ **Step Three** I now move on to the nose and eyes. I shade the eyes using an HB pencil and radial lines around the pupil. I apply less pressure to the outer edge of the iris to give the eyes a three-dimensional quality. Then I use a blunt 2B pencil to shade the nose area, avoiding the highlights around the nostrils and on the tip. I also darken the ridge in the middle of the nose and the area beneath the nostrils.

▶ **Step Four** At this stage, I want to develop the character in the eyes, so I move on to the surrounding dark hair. I use a sharp 2B pencil to draw short lines spiraling away from the eyes. I reduce the pressure below and above the eyes (along the eyelids) to imply the eyelashes and curvature of the skin. I also mark some of the spots on the face, stroking in the direction of hair growth.

▶ **Step Five** Now I complete the black spots by adding the areas in reflected light. Again using a sharp 2B pencil, I draw short lines with the white of the paper showing through to create a lighter tone. I study my reference photo and ensure that my lines follow the direction of hair growth. To avoid a harsh line around the bottom of the drawing, I greatly lighten my pressure as I approach the bottom edge, fading out the tone.

▶ **Step Six** I now begin adding tone and texture to the white fur of the Dalmatian, which I accomplish in two stages (steps six and seven). First I apply a layer of 2H pencil over the entire neck and shoulders of the dog, again gradually fading out at the bottom of the drawing. I also use the 2H to create the cast shadow of the ear. Even as I block shade, I ensure that I stroke in the direction of hair growth. Any natural variations in the pencil strokes that occur only enhance the natural look of the hair. I use the same 2H to begin adding tone to the mouth, applying heavier pressure to the edges of the lips to create curvature. Then I add another spot to the dog's cheek.

▶ **Step Seven** I go back over the areas I have just shaded with a sharp pencil eraser. I apply strokes in the direction of the hair growth to bring out the lightest hairs. Slightly varying the shape, curvature, and direction of the strokes in areas will create a sense of depth and give a more natural look to the hair. I repeat this process on the ears and begin shading the cheeks.

▶ **Step Eight** Now I work on the white fur of the face. Because the fur is white, I don't need to worry too much about detail—only rough shading is required, as any detail would be lost in this light tone. Using the blunt side of a 2H pencil, I follow the direction of hair growth and shade below the eye and down the side of the muzzle. I also add the subtle ridge on the forehead and shade along the back of the head, where less light is hitting the coat. Then I lightly shade the area above the nose and around the mouth. The whisker markings are quite subtle, so I suggest them simply using dots and an H pencil. Finally, I return with the 2H to shade between the markings, implying separation of hair in this area.

Maine Coon

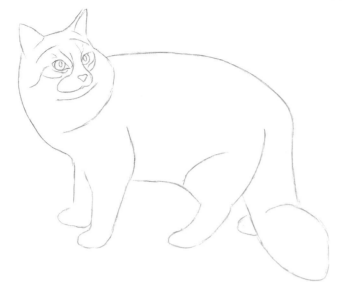

Step One I begin sketching the general shape of the cat. This cat has an interesting pose; we are viewing it from the side, but its head is turned, looking behind and slightly upward. With this in mind, I shift the position of the cat to the left side of the paper. This creates a more dynamic composition and encourages the viewer to wonder what the cat is looking at.

Step Two As always, I fine tune the outlines until I have a detailed line drawing to work with. This fine tuning includes defining the features and the markings of the cat's coat. I also indicate the pupils, guiding the cat's gaze so that it appears to look directly into the vacant space behind it—I am not too concerned with the markings on the body—I will address these during the shading stage.

Step Three I begin shading the head first, as this will be the more taxing area of this drawing. I block in the black areas of the eyes and nose, as well as the darkest markings of the cat's head. I simply create short and dark lines with a 2B pencil, making sure to follow the direction of hair growth.

Step Four Switching to a slightly lighter HB pencil, I further develop the markings of the head. The cat's eyes are relatively dark, so I use the HB pencil and light pressure to block shade the eyes; then I apply more pressure as I add radial lines. I also create the eyelid's cast shadow along the top of each eye. Then I block in the nose, darkening it slightly toward the bottom and sides to suggest its form.

Step Five To finish the head, I first indent the whiskers with a blunt but fine metal point; then I apply a light layer of graphite over the entire area using an H pencil and avoiding only the white of the muzzle and the white fur surrounding the eyes. I then apply texture within the fur by overlaying short strokes using an HB pencil. The coat should lighten around the neck, so I change to a blunt H pencil as I move down. To finish the head, I first indent the whiskers with a blunt but fine metal point; then I apply a light layer of graphite over the entire area.

Step Six After finishing the fur on the neck, I tackle the darks of the rest of the cat in one go. I begin by picking out the darkest areas of fur using a 2B pencil and a series of lines in the direction of hair growth. To create the area where the lighter neck fur lays over the dark fur, I first block in the area and then erase the overlaying hairs. As the light source is in front of the cat, most of the darkest fur is on the backs of the legs, body, and tail. Note that the fur on the legs is shorter in length than on the body—with this in mind, I keep my pencil strokes shorter in these areas.

Step Seven I now block shade the entire body using a blunt HB pencil, avoiding only the fronts of the legs, the light fur at the top of the hind leg, and the end of the tail that is catching the light. Although I am only block shading at this stage, I still follow the direction of hair growth. This ensures that if any of my shading pencil strokes show through at the end, they will only enhance the appearance of fur.

▶ **Step Eight** To further develop the coat, I go back over the entire body with a sharp 2B pencil, applying lines in the direction of hair growth. I randomly create areas where my lines are closer together and areas where they are farther apart to give the appearance of natural partings and clumps within the coat. I work dark lines into the lighter areas for texture; then I use an eraser to create random light hairs and define the light patch on the hind leg.

◀ **Step Nine** Finally, to ground the cat and provide a sense of space in the drawing, I apply a layer of H pencil below the body and feet using horizontal strokes. I am not creating a shadow—rather, I am creating the appearance of ground that continues behind the cat.

OCICAT

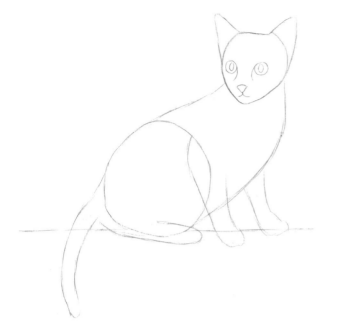

Step One I begin by sketching the rough position of the cat. I plan to place the cat on a wall with its tail hanging down, so I mark this wall by placing a horizontal line a third of the way up the paper. I draw a large circle on the line for the cat's rear and a smaller circle for the cat's head. I join the two circles with sweeping lines to indicate the chest and back. I also add the ears, which helps show the direction of the cat's head. I expand on my outline drawing by adding the front and rear legs, the tail, and the facial features, adjusting the shapes to match my reference.

Step Two Now that I have a rough idea of position and proportion, I erase my rough drawing almost completely and create a detailed line drawing on top. I fine-tune the features and delineate the main markings of the cat's coat. I also sketch the wall beneath the cat. Notice that the bricks are not simply rectangles—they are irregular and cracked.

Step Three To begin shading, I pick out all the black areas of the cat. These include the pupils, nostrils, and black markings all over the body. I simply block in some areas, such as the pupils, using a 2B pencil—but the black areas on the coat need to have more form. I indicate these areas using very short lines in the direction of hair growth. Note how these markings are farther apart across the back where the coat is stretched but closer together around the hind leg where the fur collects.

Step Four I now start filling in the features and the face. I apply a layer of graphite using an H pencil over the eyes and nose, leaving highlights in the eyes. I then draw radial lines out from the pupil to create the textured look of a cat's eye. The fur of the face is very short, so I use a sharp HB pencil to draw short lines up from the nose, out around the eyes and over the top of the head. Layered over the black areas of the fur, these lines create the midtone. I leave the white of the paper showing through to indicate the lighter fur above and below the eyes.

Step Five I now block shade the entire cat. Using an H pencil, I cover the cat with a single layer of graphite, avoiding only the white chin and the area around the nose. I then apply a second layer over the cat, this time avoiding the lighter chest and fronts of the legs. I slightly darken the insides of the ears; then I erase the stray white hairs that grow over the ears.

Step Six With roughly the right tones in place, I create the texture of the body. Using a sharp HB pencil, I apply short lines over the body following the direction of hair growth. I use more pressure in the shadow areas, such as under the haunches and around the shoulder. To add texture to the paws, I greatly shorten my strokes. I also apply texture to the lighter chest and underside using an H pencil. I finish the cat by erasing the whiskers using an electric eraser. Then I move to the wall, filling in the cement using small, circular strokes and an HB. I lighten my pressure as I move down the wall, fading to create a soft edge.

◄ **Step Seven** I apply a base layer with an H pencil over the entire wall area, lightening the pressure as I move down. I then switch back to the HB pencil and apply random darker areas, creating cracks and ridges. I am careful not to allow the wall to be too dark or detailed, as it may distract the viewer's attention from the cat. To finish, I add cast shadows on the wall for the tail and legs.

LABRADOR RETRIEVER

Step One As I want this drawing to be a very detailed and lifelike portrait, I use the grid method to create my line drawing. (See steps one, two, and three on page 16.) Once I have my detailed outline in place, I immediately dive into detailed shading. Using a 2B pencil, I apply tone in the darkest areas: the pupils, the skin surrounding the eyes, the edges of the nostrils, and the mouth area. I move on to the nose using an HB pencil, drawing very small circles and varying the size and pressure to suggest the form. I am careful to leave the tops and sides of the nose white where the light is reflecting. In this case, the insides of the nostrils aren't black—the light is reflecting within.

Step Two To complete the nose, I use an HB pencil to apply a layer of slightly larger circles over the entire nose, toning down the highlights and adding texture. I also apply dark shading below the nose with a 2B pencil. As I move outward, I draw short lines that converge to a point, suggesting gaps between the light hairs. Before addressing the mouth's interior, I indent whiskers and hairs along the upper lip. Then I use the 2B pencil to add tone to the gums, giving them a smooth and moist look by leaving small specks of white. Now I shade the tongue with an HB pencil. I use this shadow to suggest its form, curving the shadow over the tongue's surface.

Step Three I now begin to work on the fur. A Labrador has a short, yellow coat, so I will render it almost exclusively using a sharp HB pencil and short strokes that follow the direction of hair growth. I leave quite a lot of white paper showing through my lines to keep the fur light. To change the tone, I simply apply the lines closer together or farther apart to create darker or lighter areas. To make the rest of the head a little less daunting, I look for darker areas of fur, such as around the ears, and shade these first. This breaks up the space and creates smaller areas to work on.

Step Four From the muzzle, I continue up and over the top of the head with the HB, taking the hair back and out toward the ears. I leave the bridge of the muzzle and the area above the eyes almost completely white, as this is where the light is hitting the dog's head directly. I apply very few light lines with a 2H pencil to indicate some hair here.

Step Five I work on the ears in two stages. In stage one, I create the texture of the ears using an HB pencil. I make a ridge at the inner edge of the ear where it folds slightly. I curve my lines around the edges of the ear, giving the impression that the coat continues on the other side. The light on the left ear is strong, so I leave it almost completely white.

Step Six In stage two, I simply apply an even layer of HB pencil over the ears, making sure that I don't apply too much pressure—I don't want this layer to be as dark as the lines I laid in the first stage. A Labrador's ears are generally darker than its body, so I also blend the area with a tissue until I reach the desired shade. I use the same two-stage method (laying in lines with an HB pencil, then shading over the top) for the area directly below the mouth.

◀ **Step Seven** Now I work on the collar. There are just two textures here to re-create—the fabric band and the buckle. First I indent strands of hair over the band to protect them from tone. Then I lay down ridges along the band using parallel lines and a 2B pencil. To give the ridges form, I lightly shade to the left of each line. I finish the band by applying a layer of HB pencil over it. The metal buckle is slightly more intricate. I add the sharp edges with a 2B pencil and shade over the entire area with an H pencil. I lift out highlights with a kneaded eraser. You can see that I have extended the highlight slightly beyond the actual buckle— this makes it appear to really shine. Once I finish the buckle, I create the coat below the neck. First I add a layer of H pencil, blending the strokes with a tissue. Then I go over the area with an HB pencil, stroking in the directions of hair growth. To keep the viewer's focus on the head, I fade out gradually along the bottom for a soft, subtle edge.

About the Artist

Nolon Stacey is a self-taught graphite artist who specializes in the realistic fine art drawings of dogs, rural scenery, farm animals, and wildlife. Having never had any formal art training, Nolon acquired the methods he uses through trial and error. As a child in South Yorkshire, England, Nolon cultivated his interest in drawing throughout school. He eventually earned a degree in mathematics from Warwick University, but he soon returned to his artistic passion and began specializing in human and canine portraits. Nolon currently lives in North Yorkshire surrounded by the inspirational Yorkshire countryside. Working as a full-time graphite artist, Nolon publishes and sells prints of his extensive dog breed collection and rural landscapes internationally.